'HEY! I AM YOUR FRIEND IF YOU HAVE DEPRESSION'

Lavanya Agarwal

BlueRose Publishers
NewDelhi • London

First Published in January 2022

ISBN: 978-93-5472-725-2

BLUEROSE PUBLISHERS
www.bluerosepublishers.com
info@bluerosepublishers.com
+91 8882 898 898

Cover Design:
Soniya Subramanian

Typographic Design:
Ilma Mirza

Editor:
Soniya Subramanian

Distributed by: BlueRose, Amazon, Flipkart

DEDICATED TO MY DAUGHTERS

ACKNOWLEDGEMENT

My sincere thanks to my family who helped me survive.

My sincere thanks to every guru who has helped me be stronger every single day.

LAVANYA

PREFACE

This book is about having a positive approach towards life even when you are walking in the path of depression. A woman who wants to be your friend especially if you have depression and longing for a hand of love and care. Words of wisdom from few well-known gurus to soothe your mind and lead a peaceful life.

Dear Friends,

I am on antidepressants for the last 15 years. Antidepressants have lots of side effects like constipation, gas, acidity, muscular pain, etc. I had three fistula surgeries due to constipation. My monthly cycle also stopped as a result of antidepressants. I put on a lot of weight due to antidepressants. Antidepressants also make you sleepy and lethargic, but still, I will have to take them as recommended by my psychiatrist Dr. Dave.

Having depression is still not accepted in Indian society. Some people might tease you and give you names, also say that you have become mad. I was taunted, teased, called 'half-mad' who neither can be put in the mental hospital nor can be kept in the house.

But remember, our capabilities are more than our shortcomings, have faith. During the first 10years, I was so sleepy because I did not exercise at all. But after my fistula surgery, my surgeon advised me to start walking to avoid another fistula. And, I started exercising little by little and started walking too.

My friends tried to keep me busy and happy to reduce my depression. Even if you sit and scribble on a paper is better than sitting idle and thinking. When we are depressed, there is no control over our brain, and that is when there are more chances of negative thinking than positive ones. We become less optimistic and less hopeful even if some problem occurs, we or somebody falls ill for that matter.

I have regular aches and cramps on my neck, back, hands and legs. This has almost become a routine now. What helped me reduce this a bit is walking; I walk daily for 1/2 an hour both in the morning and evening. As I got used to walking daily, I realized that if I missed walking even one day, I used to think that something is missing in my life. It may differ from person to person. You can listen to music or can do anything creative while you are walking. Walking might not help you to lose weight but it can help you to not put-on excess weight. Walking will help you maintain your weight.

And now we are locked down for more than 6 months due to a pandemic, we are following it voluntarily. Sometimes I get restless at home and my anxiety increases. But writing this book has helped me to be busy. I feel very sad and depressed at times, but I keep listening to motivational videos to keep up my spirit high and learn new things about life.

I am a regular listener and follower of some well-known motivational speakers on YouTube like

Shri Gyanvatsal Swami, Shri Sandeep Maheshwari, Shri Morari Bapuji, Sister Shivani, Shri Sadhguruji Maharaj. Every time I watch their motivational videos, I feel good and elevated. I just thought I should share them with you all my dear friends, who are walking on the path of depression just like I am; hoping this makes you feel better just like I feel better.

Medication –

Ayurveda versus Allopathy Medicines

Patanjali, Dabur or Himalaya Ayurvedic medicines are better for depression rather than allopathy. I could not do it for myself but heard about many people who have been cured by Ayurvedic Medicines. Ayurvedic medicines don't have any side effects and they are not habit-forming and best for depression.

"If you can't walk a mile, walk a half, if not half,
walk a quarter, if not a quarter, just

do walk in your house or even in your room but
do the walk."

CONTENTS

Walking – an active aid

Benefits of Walking

1. Improves Circulation - Walking protects against the occurrence of any heart diseases, brings up the heart rate, lowers blood pressure, and strengthens the heart

2. Shore up your bones – Walking can stop the loss of bone mass for those suffering from osteoporosis

3. Lighten your Mood – Walking naturally reduces pain-killing endorphins of the body, also acts as one of the emotional benefits of exercise.

4. Strengthen Muscles – Walking tones your legs and abdominal muscles.

5. Improve Sleep – You get a peaceful sleep at night.

6. Support your joints – Most of the joint's cartilage has no direct blood supply. It gets

the nutrition from the joint fluid that circulates as we move. Movement from walking 'squishes' the cartilage, bringing oxygen and nutrient into that area.

7. Improve your health – When you walk your breath rate increases, causing oxygen to travel faster through the bloodstreams, which helps to eliminate waste products thus improving your energy level and ability to heal.

So, my dear friends if you don't have the habit of walking start taking baby steps now. Start with 5 minutes and then through constant practice it'll gradually increase.

Walking Strategy

Few quick strategies by Marry Anne Bunkins:

1. Find a buddy
2. Do something different
3. Get good shoes
4. Track your progress
5. Ditch the excuses

Self-Guilt –
an ephemeral feeling

I often feel very guilty after I get negative thoughts that are not under my control. So, if you feel the same then you are not alone, I am here with you dear. Many others like us are suffering from self-guilt. Even normal people get negative thoughts but they overlook them. Since we feel guilty, we keep thinking about the negative thoughts and build up our guilt more and become sad. Some people even commit suicide because of self-guilt; however, this situation can be handled by overlooking these negative thoughts. Imagine you are sitting on a bench and seeing the water waves coming to the shore and going back to the sea. Just like the waves, the negative thoughts keep coming and going. Imagine how beautiful it would be if instead of getting involved in our negative thoughts and giving way to the increasing self-guilt you start doing something else and divert your mind by getting busy. The negative thoughts just disappear and you feel good yourself.

We should not get too involved with the negative thoughts instead just watch them from far and start doing something positive. Remember and try to overcome it as normal people do. Just like I am writing this book sitting at home during the lockdown. Due to this pandemic, whenever I used to feel sad, I used to eat 'Phuchkaa' and felt nice. I would go to malls to shop, eat, watch movies and distract my mind to feel better. Do things that help your mind get busy and keep you occupied without any negative thoughts coming in.

During the initial days of the pandemic, it got difficult because I couldn't go anywhere and I used to be at home 24X7. That is when I wrote a book on mehndi designs and now, I write this book for you my dear friends. Sadness is the major reason for depression. Even though if everything around us might be going well, we still experience extreme sadness. When normal people become sad and something good happens in their life, they overcome the sadness and live happily. However, for those under depression whatever happens, no matter how good it is, the sadness doesn't fade that soon.

You tend to lose interest in all activities and even that is a sign of depression. I was a very good cook and enjoyed cooking before, but after depression, I lost all my interest in cooking. However, instead of being idle, I am trying to write books and develop some other interests to remain busy and occupied. During the depression, if something wrong happens, you tend to feel guilty and start blaming and cursing yourself. You also feel an extreme loss of energy within and often feel very tired. For example, you want to have some tea and got to make it yourself, but you feel you can't make it and you can't get up from the bed being very dull. But dear, this is the time to take some baby steps. Build up your courage slowly and start making tea for the first time, then you will make it the second time, and automatically you will overcome the fear and tiredness of making tea. Just like this try to do activities that interest you and slowly you will see that change in yourself my dear.

Poor constipation is also one of the major problems of depression. But you will have to make efforts to come over it. Never feel ashamed of having depression. People often feel guilty that are weak that they are going through depression. But it happens to anybody regardless of being strong or weak. Don't feel bad about yourself. Stop all those negative thinking about yourself and start loving yourself to raise your confidence level. It is a sickness like any other sickness, nothing less nothing more. There are ways through which you can control them and get yourself in a state of being normal again.

Following are few ways that you can do to help yourself fight against it.

Ways of Control

Finding the right counselor for yourself. When you experience a bad mood without any reason, it is important to psychologically feel good, thereby understanding there can be control over it.

Pure thoughts and impure thoughts. At times knowingly or unknowingly our thoughts become impure with negativity, but we have to forget and try to erase such impure thoughts and make them pure.

Finding the right counselor for yourself - In case you need counseling, make sure that the counselor is good. Make a thorough research about the counselor before you take an appointment. If the counselor gives you any negative counseling you can be in big trouble. Generally, old aged experienced counselors are good as they have seen and experienced all good and bad in life. When you are in depression

your mood can be bad without any reason. So,

my friends, don't worry if you are experiencing it, because I experience it too. Keep yourself busy in some activities, like simple drawing and coloring which can brighten up your mood. It's not important which activity you do but doing something is very much important. Slowly as you get involved in some activity you will realize that psychologically to feel good is in your own hands. Do some physical activity little-by-little and start reducing the aches and pains from your body. Very slowly and steadily move ahead, it's just a small start step that is to be taken.

Like I said before, I like to watch motivational videos that help me soothe my mind and be positive. I would like to share some of those points with you which will be useful to you all, just like it has been for me.

Shri Sadhguru Ji

I follow Shri Sadhguru Ji a lot, and he says even if you sit for three hours in erect posture after eating it is a form of yoga. He says heaven is right here, we people are heaven but it is us who is messing it up. Listening to Sadhguru Ji has brought a very positive impact in my life, hence I am sharing it with you all. If we eat a sattvic (pure, balanced, and most nutritious) diet we will be less angry and irritable and experience calmness and mental clarity. On the other hand, tamasic (red meat, alcohol, etc.) and rajasic (eggs, coffee, etc.) food will increase anger, irritability, ego and build more negative thoughts which are not good for health and mind both. He also says, in the morning when you get up from sleep try to turn towards the right side and get up because the heart is on the left side. After you get up, rub both your hands together and keep them on your eyes. Be happy that you are alive and smile for it. In the morning remember to first smile. We should learn to take care of our thoughts and emotions says, Shri Sadhguru Ji.

Shri Morari Bapu

As per Shri Morari Bapu's sayings:

1. As soon as you get up in the morning don't be grumpy, as mornings are to enjoy nature's beauty.

2. Whenever you go out of the house for work or any other thing, never shout at anybody.

3. Never eat food in anger, but be grateful before and after having the food.

4. After returning home back from the office or anywhere, don't be angry

    because your family has been waiting for you all day.

5. When you go to sleep do not be angry at anyone. Who knows will we be able to see tomorrow or not? Be relaxed, calm, and happy that the day is over and go to sleep peacefully.

6. Anger burns and decays the person from inside.

7. Whenever there is any problem try to sort it out with patience and explain to the other person in a soft tone.

8. Anger leads to various diseases and body problems and illness.

9. "aap ke mehfil mein log kam na honge, magar aap ki mehfil mein ham naa honge." (There will be no fewer people at your party, but I will not be there at your party.)

Shri Sanjay Raval

According to Shri Sanjay Raval sir, his sayings are as follows:

1. Jo hai, wo hai (What is there, is there!)

2. Kasrat karnaa Dharm aur Karm hai Sarvashresth. (Exercising religion and action is the best)

3. When God gives, he gives in abundance.

4. Do your best in what you do.

5. Don't worry about what you can't do.

6. God has decided your life partner at the time of your birth and it cannot be changed.

7. Love is how you are, how you were, and how you will be, I shall love you unconditionally.

8. When you think of committing suicide, think of your parents and family, how hard they worked to raise you.

9. Even if you commit suicide, you will have to go through all life's struggles all over

10. again in your rebirth.

Shri Gyanvatsal Swami

I watch videos of Shri Gyanvatsal Swami from Shri Swami Narayan BAPS Organisation and temple. He is a very good motivational speaker, and below are some of his thoughts.

1. Think win-win, let him win and I will also win

2. Do not compromise on quality

3. All the donkeys run but they don't become horses

4. If you will respect time; time will respect you

5. Whatever good or bad is happening with you, accept it as a will of god

6. Think why the other person is behaving wrongly, try to find out the reason behind it.

7. Seek first to understand and then be understood

8. Life is a compromise; life is an adjustment, keep your nature compromising

9. Sharpen your saw. Take care of your physical body.

1. There should be 25 people in your life with whom you should learn to compromise and adjust. Even if they lie, you should think it through. That level of acceptance you must have for these 25 people in life.

2. We live complaining, we are born crying and we die of no satisfaction from life.

3. We have to accept that 25 to 50 people in our life are for our benefit. We need to maintain good relations with them as we need these people in our life.

4. Don't take your family for granted. Spending quality time with your near and dear

5. ones is very necessary for any family.

6. Speak the positive language. Attitude is everything. Keep your attitude high and nice.

7. If a character is gone everything is gone.

8. If you don't do anything wrong your whole life, and your character will be

9. maintained.

10. Having a big heart and letting things go will keep you stress-free. To let go and to control your tongue from harsh words is a must for peace.

11. Anything in excess is a prison.

12. Have faith, don't ever think about suicide.

Think that all people in this world have

13. problems and you are not alone.

14. If you live a life of good character all good will come to your life automatically.

15. In the 21st century, after B. Com you need the degree of B. Calm.

16. Be cool, be steady and let the moment pass. No matter how much knowledge you have, if you get disturbed very often, you are not smart.

17. You should know how to deal with difficult situations in your life.

18. When your daughter gets married tell her to stay calm noticing the behavioral habits and lifestyle of her in-laws for at least 2 years and then be adjustable to live with them without any hustle.

19. A lady has to be tolerant, adjusting and compromising to adjust with her in-laws.

20. We have to give respect to elders.

21. In Indian culture even if we are right and elders are wrong, we should not back answer them instead politely make them understand later to avoid any argument.

22. God is doing everything and he is doing it for our good.

23. Whatever has happened, is happening, and will happen is according to

24. almighty's wish. It was, is, and will be good, just have trust and faith.

25. Fall and failure are a part of life.

26. You should spend quality time with your family.

27. The purity of character is important.

28. Mobile was made to give us service, but now we have become the servants of mobile. If every three minutes we don't touch the mobile phone we become discharged.

29. Mobile addiction is a new problem now.

30. WhatsApp takes away our time, energy and it has made us its slave from early morning till late in the night. Everybody is on WhatsApp or any other social media

31. Make a habit of not touching your phone during dinner time with your family.

32. Even if we are right and our loved or dear ones are wrong and speaks wrong against us, we have to learn to bear with it.

33. Work-life balance is a must. The greatest joy upon this earth is spending your quality time with your near and dear ones whom you love and respect just as they love and respect you.

34. Charity is good for everybody regardless of little or more, one should always do.

35. Sometimes circumstances also create stress.

36. A stress-free life is not possible for any human

being.

37. Stress is an enviable part of life.

38. At the end of the day, man is the bundle of his thoughts.

39. Social service is good for everybody.

40. Selfless service gives you happiness and contentment.

41. In the joy of others lies our own.

42. The attitude should be big and positive to enjoy your life.

43. Adjustment is life.

44. Compromise is life.

45. Adjustment and compromise should be the attitude of life.

46. To keep yourself stable is the first important aspect of life.

47. Seek first to understand and then be understood.

48. If you are ethically right your foundation for success is strong.

49. 80% of the reasons for your success are the values and virtues of your life.

50. Think right and think rationally.

51. Your words build up your personality.

52. Speak thoughtfully.

53. The head is thinking, the mouth is speaking, and the hands are working. Your action speaks louder than your words and thinking.

54. Act purposefully and speak thoughtfully.

55. A selfless attitude is good thinking for the betterment of everybody.

56. Our character should be so pure that we must inspire the future generation.

57. Don't fear hard work. You cannot go to the top with an elevator, it is always a

58. staircase.

59. 24 hours are like the 8+8+8 hours division of the day. The first 8 hours should be for work and duties. The next 8 hours for 3 F - family, friends, and faith, 3 H – Health, Hygiene, and Hobby, and 3 S – Soul, Service, Smile. Next 8 hours rest and sleep.

60. 24 hours classified as per the below:

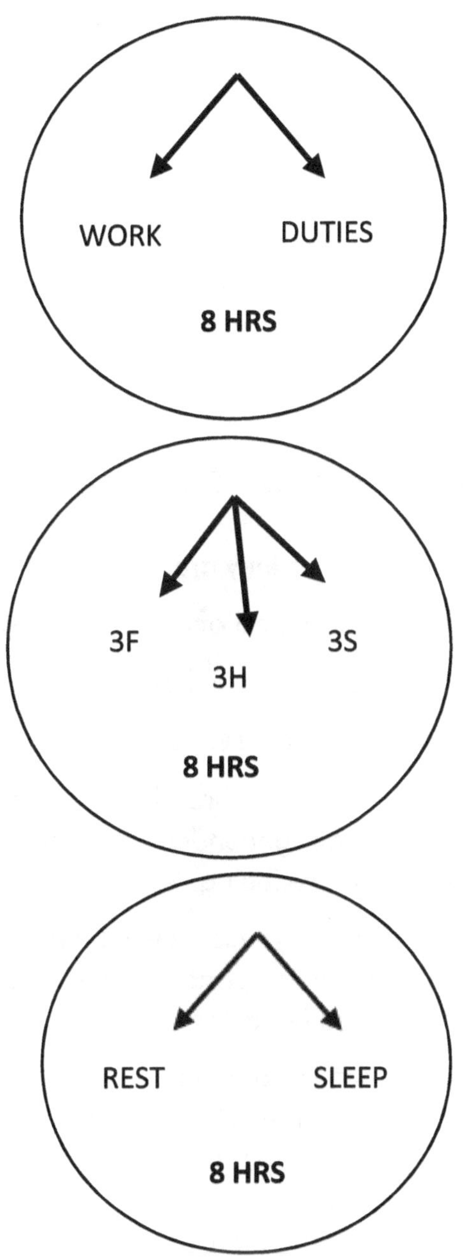

WORK
DUTIES
8 HRS
3F
3H
3S
8 HRS
REST
SLEEP
8 HRS

Brahma Kumari Sister Shivani

As per Brahma Kumari Shivani sister's sayings:

1. I accept people as they are.

2. Let go of anger, let go of criticism.

3. People will accept me as I am.

4. Protect yourself every single day.

5. When we get disturbed by someone's behavior, we get dependent on other outside sources for our wellbeing.

6. The law of the universe never blesses us nor punish us. It only responds to the vibration of our attitude and behavior.

7. Everything that is happening in our life is an energy that we attract. It is a consequence of previous energy sent by us. At times these consequence returns after a long gap or maybe in our next birth, but whatever comes

to us is a return of what we have sent earlier.

8. We often feel bad when people do not behave the right way with us, they cheat, betray and reject us. We have thoughts about why do they behave this way even when we are good to them. But we only know our behavior with them in this life, there could have been times where we might have behaved differently in our earlier births. The energy that we receive from them is the return of our karma with the soul of our previous birth.

9. When we do not remember that people's such behavior is the return of our past energy that we'd sent

10. to them, then we blame them, criticize them further making way to hatred and build negative energy once again. If we take personnel responsible for the energy that we are receiving today, we consciously send only blessings and good wishes this time.

According to Brahma Kumari, writing the below sentences/phrases 21 times for 21 days can lead to peace of mind

- "Silence ends quarrels". I write this regularly even today

- "I am a peaceful soul"

- "I have to be humble and love everybody"

- "Your one sound of anger can destroy your future"

- "Time is my friend and it will support me"

  The above assertive can be written for the said period or you may continue it till the time you want. It helps you to feel better every time you feel bad.

1. We should take care of our mind in this time of COVID crisis

2. Increase your emotional fitness

3. Learn to emotionally train yourself

4. Think positive, Meditate

5. First, you must understand other people then expect to be understood

6. Watch, Eat, Drink and Listen. These things should be with high energy as we intake all these

7. If you want to be emotionally strong, spend the first 60 minutes of your day in the morning taking care of your inner world

8. Every early morning, listen to the good things which make you emotionally stronger

9. Say this to yourself, "I am a peaceful, patient soul. Patience is my nature."

10. "I am emotionally independent of energies, people, and situation."

Shri Sandeep Maheshwari

Mentally Strong by Sandeep Maheshwari. I am a great fan of Sir Sandeep Maheshwari and watch his motivational videos regularly on YouTube. He helps us understand how to be mentally strong like:

1. Physically strong means muscles are strong and mentally strong means

2. When some problems come in our life, we can understand through our thinking muscles whether they give up or overcome the problem.

3. When we overthink, we get stuck in our thinking. So basically, we are not stuck in a problem but our thinking. So, we have to find a way out when we are stuck in our thought process.

4. Don't think too much but think right. You have to think scientifically to get out

of any problem.

5. Seeing the reality as it is, is a scientific approach to any problem.

6. Try to observe life as life and not as 'my life'. If we see the objective, in reality, we cannot be stuck anywhere. We have to see the causes of our failures and then can see the reality.

7. When somebody is in some problem we should empower and inspire the person to come out of it.

8. When the body is fit, the mind becomes peaceful. Mind and body are not different from each other, they are the same.

9. Planning is a work of the intellect. Execution is a work of your emotions. The energy in motion is emotion. Don't fight with your emotion but try to divert them into your desired action by telling yourself a story.

10. We have to learn to accept both success and failure because both are not permanent.

11. Understand that your thoughts are working on your mind.

12. There are unlimited thoughts in our minds and we keep thinking about the past and future.

13. Live in the present.

14. You have to make effort to remain positive, we

are always flowing an inflow of negative thoughts.

15. Focus on your brain and thoughts, control is in your own hands, use it like an on/off switch.

16. The thought is nothing but a word, language, and information.

17. Language is only thought. We do less and think more.

18. Language has evolved and become complex. Language is just for communication.

19. Everything has a role so does the thought. And language is for communication. It's like you cannot do make-up with a mobile phone but you can learn to do the make-up with the mobile phone.

20. Use your thoughts only when you want to do any work. Otherwise, do not use them only then can you say that you have full control over your mind.

21. A thoughtless state is amazing if you can reach that level.

22. A thoughtless state gives us rest and nature heals everything.

23. Look at language or thought as a tool that is to be used when something has to be done. That's it. Use a thought when you want to do something or learn something.

24. Don't use thoughts in the wrong way, you have to understand the significance of language and put it in the right place in your life. You have to learn to control your mind.

25. The deeper you understand this, you will have more control over your mind and you will be in a thoughtless state for the maximum time.

26. Memory is good for learning, not for suffering.

27. When you know how to use your thought you will be free from your psychological fear.

28. Gratitude changes everything.

29. Emotional pain does not go easily. All your memories are put together in you. The brain's work is to store memories. It is normal for the brain to repeat those memories. It is up to us to end all the bad memories and cherish the good ones.

30. It's ok if the brain repeats bad memories, we just underestimate our capacity that we cannot take those memories but actually we can and our body will take it willingly.

31. No matter how many bad things a person has faced, that many good things

    will also come on his life's journey.

32. Be open to anything and everything. Everybody goes through failures. The brain has lots of possibilities.

33. Bad memories come and go, so do not get involved with them. See them like water waves that come on the shore and go back to the sea. You just have to be normal.

34. You are stronger than you think and one day that bad memory will be simply be deleted from your mind.

35. Anger is not like nature's call that comes naturally. We knowingly get angry at

    somebody.

36. We should take responsibility for our anger and knowingly try to control it too.

37. We should not react without thinking. We should understand, think and then react. This will stop overreaction.

38. First, clear your mind then go to learn the world.

39. Take a gap, observe the things, and keep your mind cool and clear.

40. Thought is just an illusion.

41. Speak to yourself or listen to the below sentences every night before you sleep:

- Today was great

- I did my best

- I am satisfied

- I am calm

- Today was better

- Tomorrow will be the best

- I am fearless

- I am limitless

- I am free

- Universe is with me

- I am thankful

- I am different

- I am powerful

- I am blissful

- I am sincere

- Success will happen

- I breathe positively

- All is good

- I am enlightened

- I love all

- I forgive all

- I forgive myself

- I think about a new start

- I am ready for tomorrow

- I thank all

- I believe in myself

- Everyone loves me

- I am happiness

- It's time to rest

- Be peaceful

42. Sir also talks about Chanakya neeti and says being good is nice but not so much that someone takes you the advantage and fool you again and again.

43. When any thought comes to your mind first thing should give importance to it or not. If it is negative let it pass because if mind id there thought will come and go.

44. Let go of the negative thought. Don't be angry.

45. Mind mapping helps.

46. We get scared by our imagination.

47. Let us face the fear of our imagination. We have to fight it. Face the fear and it goes away.

Cooking - a therapy

Another way of reducing your stress is COOKING. Your interest in cooking will keep your mind steady and revive your mood completely.

Here are a few recipes for you to try in your kitchen and indulge in the goodness of healthy cooking.

Rajma Kabab

In a bowl, take one cup of boiled rajma (added salt). Add ¼ cup of turmeric powder, ½ tsp of dhaniya powder, ¼ tsp salt, 2 tsp besan, fresh green dhaniya leaves. Mix and mash everything together. Put it on the tava / hot pan adding some ghee and cook on both sides till it turns to a golden brown. Serve hot with green chutney.

Mix Rice Cutlets

Add 1 cup of cooked rice and ½ cup curd mix

well together. Take ½ cup of sooji and ½ cup of curd and mix well. Combine both the mixture and add salt to taste. Then form a shape like a donut or medu vada and serve with coconut chutney. You can put green chillies (optional) and coriander leaves also in the cutlet mixture.

Vegetable Biryani

First, boil the rice and keep it aside. Slice some vegetables like carrots, French beans, cauliflower and marinate them in hung curd so that the water is left in curd. Add masalas such as turmeric powder, salt, dhaniya powder, red chili powder and mix it well. Keep it aside for ½ an hour. Take a pan and cook all the marinated vegetables on a medium flame. Then take some ghee, milk, and Kesar in a hot pan and make a mixture. In a bowl first, add the rice and vegetables in layers one over another. Pour the mixture of liquids on the top. Cook it for 20 minutes at 180°C.

Paneer Tikka

Take some diced pieces of capsicum, tomato, onion, yellow capsicum, and marinate in hung curd. Add some turmeric powder, dhaniya powder, red chili powder, garam masala, and marinate for 2 hrs. On a skewer or wooden stick layer the vegetables and paneer in your desired order and roast it on the pan adding some ghee and butter. Cook until golden brown and serve it hot with green chutney and sliced raw onion.

Rajasthani Dal

Take 5 tablespoon chana dal, ½ cup moong dal. Wash them together well. On a pressure cooker add the dal mixture along with some salt, turmeric, water and put it to boil. Then take a kadhai to add some jeera, tomato, hing, coriander leaves, and salt. Combine this mixture into the dal. First, add ghee followed by hing and jeera, then add red chili powder, finely chopped tomatoes, and a pinch of garam masala and coriander leaves. Add all this to the dal and boil it for 5 minutes. Serve hot. Add some salt and lemon for taste.

Dry Moong Dal

In a bowl take 1 cup moong dal, wash and boil it with salt and turmeric and keep aside. Then in a kadhai take some ghee and add some hing, jeera, tomatoes, red chili, garam masala, salt. Sauté until tomatoes cook well. Then add dal into the masala and dry moong dal is ready. Add some salt and lemon for taste.

Cauliflower Soup

Cut the cauliflower into florets, finely chopped onions, and carrots. In a vessel take some ghee, add the veggies, add salt and water, and put it to boil. After it is boiled set it aside to cool. Now churn the mixture adding little hot milk and make a soup consistency. Sprinkle some black pepper salt to taste and serve hot. Can add coriander leaves for garnish if you like.

Pasta Bread

Add some olive oil and butter to a hot pan. Then add garlic, oregano, chili flakes, finely chopped carrot, cabbage, French beans, and some salt. Let it cook for some time, then add tomatoes into this mixture and add cheese on the top bringing it to a boil. Finally, add pav bread into the mixture and microwave it. As soon as the mixture mixes with pav bread immediately remove it from the oven.

Mexican Rice

For Mexican Masala

- ½ tsp cumin powder

- ¾ tsp coriander powder

- 1 tsp oregano powder

- Salt as per taste
- 1 red chilli powder For Salsa
- 4 medium tomatoes
- 1 big onion (chopped)
- 2 green chilli (chopped)
- 3 tsp coriander powder
- Salt to taste
- 1 tsp lemon juice For Nachos
- 1 cup wheat flour
- ½ cup corn flour
- 1 tsp prepared Mexican masala
- Oil for shallow frying For Mexican Rice
- 1 tsp oil
- 2 garlic cloves finely chopped
- 1 medium chopped onion
- ¼ cup carrot, peeled and chopped
- ¼ cup chopped capsicum
- ¼ cup boiled kidney beans
- ½ cup tomato puree
- 3 tsp Mexican masala
- 2 cups cooked rice

- Salt as per taste

- ¼ cup chopped tomatoes

- 2 tsp finely chopped green coriander leaves
  For Mexican Masala Mix

- 1½ tsp cumin powder

- ¾ tsp coriander powder

- 1 tsp oregano powder

- 1 tsp chilli powder

- Salt as per taste

For salsa, add onion in tomato puree, add lemon juice, coriander leaves, salt, and chili.

For nachos, make a dough, flatten the dough like a roti using a rolling pin. Cut them into small triangular shapes and shallow fry in oil.

For Mexican rice, heat oil in a pan, add chopped garlic, onion, carrot, capsicum, chilly green, and keep in a medium flame until all vegetables are cooked well. Then add tomato puree and finely chopped tomatoes and stir a little. Add the rice and garnish with 3 tsp masala salt and stir well, serve hot. Lastly, add some gloated cheese on the top if you like it.

Sooji Ladoo

- 1 cup sooji
- ¼ cup ghee
- 1 cup sugar powder
- 1 cup malai

Add ghee to a pan and roast the sooji until lightly golden brown on a medium flame. Then add malai and sugar and stir a little and cover for 5 minutes. Remove in thali add some dry fruits (optional), keep aside for some time then form into round shapes and make ladoo when it is slightly warm. It can be stored for 8 to 10 days and will stay fresh.

Hara Bhara Kabab

Blanch the spinach leaves with some pinch of salt. Boil 1 cup chana dal and grind it into a paste. Then in a pan add ghee, ginger-garlic paste and add the dal paste that has been made before and keep it aside. Take the palak and grind it into a paste. Add the palak paste into the previously made mixture adding some salt to taste, jeera powder, garam masala, little lemon juice and combine them all. Now make small kabab-shaped rounds and flatten them. On a pan add some ghee and roast the kababs on both sides. Serve hot with onion slices and hung curd. Serve with salt to taste if required.

Lauki Ka Halwaa

Take one whole lauki, wash and peel off the skin, cut into halves and remove out the middle part of the seeds. Grate the lauki using a grater. Add ¼ cup ghee on a pan and sauté the lauki till it softens then add ¼ cup homemade malai and ¼ cup sugar and cook till halwa leaves out the ghee. Serve hot with toppings of dry fruits of your choice.

Along with this book, I am also writing a book on mehndi designs and while I was drawing designs, I noticed that there are endless possibilities in our life. Even with one finger design, you can create a beautiful design and it looks as pretty as filling the whole hand.

It's very beautiful to find the possibilities and embrace a happy life. Look ahead of what beautiful possibilities life has to offer and do what you love to do. Be it drawing, cooking, walking, exercising, etc. All that you do for yourself is always beautiful.